THE MAGICAL RHYMES

ISHI AGGARWAL

Her Principal Mrs. Ashu Tyagi motivated her and supported her. Because of which she was able to publish this beautiful "The Magical Rhymes" book and make everyone proud.

Mrs. Heena Gupta & Mr. Ankit Gupta

Dedicating all my work to both of you. Thank you for supporting
in my journey.
Love you mummy and papa.

Contents

Contents

About The Author

A 12-year old girl. Who loved to write poems. To get her own book published was one of her dreams. She is the youngest Author of Shamli. She used to participate in every writing competition which helped her improve her writing skills.

About The Book

"The Magical Rhymes" is all about positive, motivating and some sad poems. These poems will help you to refresh your memories. These poems will motivate you whenever you want.

Always Remember,

"Whenever You Are Feeling Alone, Don't Forget That 'The Magical Rhymes' Are Always there to help you!?"

A Book By
PENAAKI

Teachers

1. Teachers

They are the one who never betray
For us only they always pray.
I have a special place for them in my heart
As in my game of Life,
Only they helped me to start!!
For me,
They are the best present.
Also known as...
Second parent!
Each one is a gem, And I....
Salute them.
They give me ideas about right and wrong
Notice my weaknesses and make me strong.
With a special gift of learning and a heart that deeply cares,
They add a lot of love to everything I share.
They are such a special gift,
That no words can truly tell,
The more they are valued is less;
Just for the work they do so well.

Life Of College

2. Life Of College

Casuals on
Open hair,
Studying or not;
I don't care.
Not doing homework
Disobeying the teacher
Different fun...
In getting Beaten.
There will be some boys
Who might look like toys
The girls might be lazy
Acting crazy.
Eating maggi
Skipping meal,
Don't know how...
Mom will feel.

I Miss You

3. I Miss You

I love to see you
As I believe you
Come on give me a hug
I really wanna feel you
I smile from outside
Cry from inside
I really want someone
For me to guide
Come on wipe my tears
Because there is no one who cares,
Now I know how to fake smile
As I have lived for one year without my lifeline
At last just wanna say,
Without you i've become a toy of clay.
My heart is completely broken,
If you would come back,
The same couldn't happen.

I Want...

4. I Want...

Don't leave me
Because you are the key.
Yes, the key of my life;
With which everything is fine.
I love you
Love you from the bottom of my heart
I hate everyone because of the sadness,
Filled in my heart.
I want a hug
I want some love.
I really want a hand
But only have glove.
I really want some shine
On the face of mine,
Because I've already lost,
My only sunshine.
At last I just want to say,
Remembering you is easy,
I do it everyday.
Missing you is the heartache
That will never go away.

Charm in my life

5. Charm in my life

Marshmallow to my hot chocolate
Orange to my juice;
Sugar to my coffee
And calory to my food.
Square-shaped face
Which is only mine;
No. 1 in everything
Related To Crime.
She eats Dosa
With fork & knife;
Without her jokes,
Incomplete is my life.
Never the one who studies
Always the one who plays,
Atleast 5 guys are needed,
For her to praise!

MY SPECIAL TEACHER-1

6. MY SPECIAL TEACHER-1

You are my special teacher
I just want you to know,
I will always remember you
Even after i grow
Sometimes i have not been so good
Sometimes even rude,
But no matter what i've done
You always teach me so good!!
You are the special one
Who always gives his best,
And for every child who takes your class;
His/her life is truly the most blessed!!
At last i just want to say....
Thankyou for all that you do
Thank you for helping me learn more.
thank you for giving me so many skills,
Now i really know a lot more..!

Kick To My Smile

7. Kick To My Smile

Every time in full attitude
Still cares for others pain,
No matter how much we become rude,
She is always there to motivate.
Always refusing to coffee
So as being sleepy,
After making high ponytail;
Looks the most creepy.
Has a lot of anger issues
And a heart full of love
She is always called Ms. Perfect Teeth;
Just because of those beautiful canines of her
She is really very annoying
But also caring at the same time,
No matter how much angry I am...
Her jokes always make me smile...!

My Special Teacher-2

8. My Special Teacher-2

You are not just a teacher

But also, a very good friend,

After hearing your motivational talks

I become Better than anyone else

You have so much knowledge about everything

Still not a single drop of arrogance,

I just want to thank you;

For giving me so much importance..!

Sorry

9. Sorry

Sorry for loving you unconditionally
Sorry for not identifying your clever side,
Sorry for always being there for you
Sorry for not making you realise when I cried.
Sorry for giving you this much importance
Sorry for forgetting my self respect for you
Sorry for not realising...
That true lovers can get betrayed too.
Sorry for never hiding my feelings in front of you
Sorry for spending my precious time for you,
Sorry for never checking your phone...
And then not realising that you were a psycho too.
Sorry for fighting with my loved ones
Just because of your silly mistakes,
Sorry for always making you feel special
Even when you were not worthy for the same.
Sorry for not making my heart understand...
That You Are never gonna be honest to me
Sorry for crying over a stupid man like you
Who can't even complement a single cup of tea.

My True Friend

10. My True Friend

You are my true Friend.
For whom I can die,
Only the one for whom;
I can say anyone goodbye.
You are rude from outside
Caring from inside,
Your one stand-up comedy;
Can always make me smile.

I Am A Teenager

11. I Am A Teenager

I am a teenager
I am the one who fakes her smile,
I am struggling with my studies...
And even with my life.
I am a teenager
Who has become the most private with my life,
Now I don't share anything with people
For them....
I Am Always Fine..!
I am a teenager
Who is the only one who annoys,
Sometimes I feel like...
Without my presence;
Everyone enjoys!!

Shamli

12. Shamli

Come to shamli once
I promise it will feel like heaven here,
Here u will also get a chance to visit...
The most beautiful trade fair.
Hanuman Tilla is one of the best temple
Where lord Hanuman will shower all his blessings on you,
Trust me it is the best place u can ever go to...
Because except the famous lemonade everything here is brand
new.
You would love to talk to the people of Shamli
As They will always care for you,
Either they will inform you about the broken stand of your bike;
Or about the lane no. 3 in which construction is going through.
You will find the uniquest tyre here
In the carrier wheels factory,
As it is the only tyre to be made without a joint...
And is also awarded by Mr. Narendra Modi.

Day By Day

13. Day By Day

Day by day we are growing older
Day by day we are becoming mature,
Day by day we are starting to understand life
Day by day our soul is becoming pure.

Those Magical Nights

14. Those Magical Nights

Those magical stars were so bright
When It came to you and me,
But i didn't even realise...
That later on they are gonna hurt me.
Not today but tomorrow,
You are also gonna regret.
You will surely miss our very last night,
And our very last together moment.

Childhood

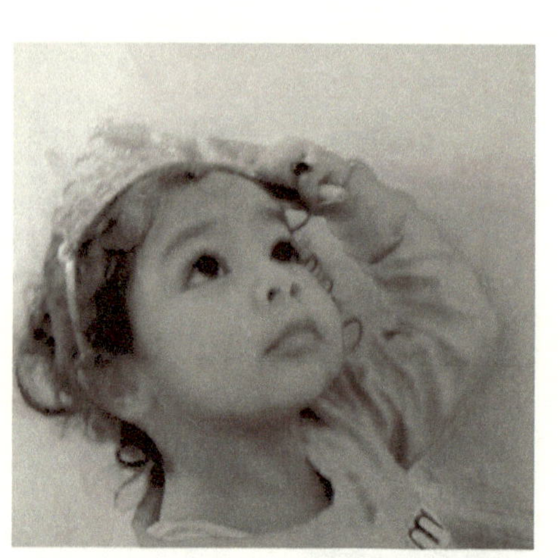

15. Childhood

Childhood is all about fun
It is all about that colorful cotton candy,
It is the only phase of time...
In which we can live
Without having
Anxiety.

Suicide

16. Suicide

It's time for me to die
It's time for you all to get rid of me,
It's time for me to say goodbye
As I also know...
You are now just bored of me!

LIFE

17. LIFE

Life is all about sacrifices
Life is all about positive thinking,
Life almost
teaches you
everything,
Like...
"Good people are as important as breathing"

Happiness

18. Happiness

Something which is very hard to find,
Something which takes our lives on rewind.
Something which will
help you to live your life with ease,
Something which you have to find for yourself,
For not just to please.
Something which no one is gonna create
But you will be the one who gonna release.
Something which makes you feel the best
Something with which people will be jealous of you,
Something with which you can confidently say....
That God will see the rest.

Depression

19. Depression

Depression is not a joke my dear,
Sometimes a person
Who is laughing on the outside can also be dead on the inside.
And sometimes a person
Who is sleeping a lot can also be depressed inside.
Better not argue with people struggling with depression
As depression can also
Be the reason for some people to commit suicide,
Because of your argument and their overthinking,
Those helpless people can't sleep at night.

Best Friend

20. Best Friend

Best friend can also break your heart
Best friend can also die for you,
Best friend can also love you till the rest of your life
And best friend can even murder you.
Be safe around your best friend
Because everyone wakes up with different feelings everyday,
Never ever trust your best friend so much...
That without him there could be
No one with whom you can be safe.

That cup of coffee

21. That cup of coffee

That cup of coffee
Which almost fixes everything
Either it's related to your studies
Or about those annoying mood swings.
That cup of coffee
Which helps you to Take out all your frustration
But always remember...
Whenever you are not able to sleep,
That cup of coffee is the only reason.

www.ingramcontent.com/pod-product-compliance
Lightning Source LLC
Chambersburg PA
CBHW022035150726
47990CB00002B/977